SPOOKY SAGAS

SOMERSET

Edited By Wendy Laws

First published in Great Britain in 2019 by:

Young Writers

Young Writers
Remus House
Coltsfoot Drive
Peterborough
PE2 9BF
Telephone: 01733 890066
Website: www.youngwriters.co.uk

All Rights Reserved
Book Design by Camilla Davis
© Copyright Contributors 2019
SB ISBN 978-1-78988-217-9
Printed and bound in the UK by BookPrintingUK
Website: www.bookprintinguk.com
YB0395N

YoungWriters Est. 1991

YOUNG WRITERS INFORMATION

We hope you have enjoyed reading this book – and that you will continue to in the coming years.

If you're a young writer who enjoys reading and creative writing, or the parent of an enthusiastic poet or story writer, do visit our website www.youngwriters.co.uk. Here you will find free competitions, workshops and games, as well as recommended reads, a poetry glossary and our blog. There's lots to keep budding writers motivated to write!

If you would like to order further copies of this book, or any of our other titles, then please give us a call or order via your online account.

Young Writers
Remus House
Coltsfoot Drive
Peterborough
PE2 9BF
(01733) 890066
info@youngwriters.co.uk

Join in the conversation!
Tips, news, giveaways and much more!

YoungWritersUK   @YoungWritersCW

THE PEOPLE WHO RIDE SCOOTERS

Me and Daniel went to my house to play the Xbox. We decided to go on our scooters. We were riding our scooters, looking for somewhere to sit. Ten minutes later, we sat down and were talking until we went to sleep. Me and Daniel heard something coming inside the woods. We went closer, the sound got louder. We got lost... There were trees bigger than usual and a dark silhouette ran past. We were scared. Meanwhile, we were still walking and we found an exit and daylight. We kept on walking...

Eddie Bushnell (10)
Westfield Primary School, Radstock

THE NEW HOUSE

When they got there, Max thought it looked splendid but when he got in he saw it was filthy and cobwebbed. He was very exhausted and needed a nap so he went to find a bed. When he woke up it was gloomy in his room. Then he saw little crimson eyes at the end of the bed. He screamed and ran downstairs, trying to find a way out. Whatever it was was chasing him. Weirdly, he heard little screams. Eventually, he got out. He only stopped when he reached his new school. Nothing. Silence. "What am I gonna do?"

Harvey Bancroft (11)
Westfield Primary School, Radstock

THE FOREST MYSTERY

It was late at night, Emily wasn't tired so she tiptoed down the stairs and put on her coat and shoes and went out of the door, realising she had forgotten something. Just after, she heard a knock at the door. She looked out the window but only a red eye flickered. She got to the forest, still searching but all she could hear was a quiet hiss. She followed the sound but fell asleep dreaming of elves and goblins. When she woke up, she was chased away by a huge shadow back to her house. What was following her?

Kelsey Hiscocks (10)
Westfield Primary School, Radstock

THE HAUNTED SCHOOL

Stealthily, Donald tiptoed down the stairs so nobody would hear him. Donald eventually reached the school and went to English. Next, he had to go out to break. Donald played knights and invaders. It was there he saw a space crystal. During break he got knocked out.

Later, he woke in the classroom. His teachers were aliens. Donald ran for his life. Tables hit his chest, chairs hit his feet and pencils hit his face but he got free. He ran to the phone box to call 999 but before he got there something grabbed him...

Thomas Andrews (11)
Westfield Primary School, Radstock

LOCKED AWAY

Brooke walked downstairs to sneak out of her house. Brooke called her friend to go to a creepy house. They found a dungeon. It was blocked, with nothing but chairs so they went to sleep.

When they woke up all the lights went off, the girls heard something. The fireplace turned on. They heard a bang. An eye twitched and the girls heard a bark. They hid. Cardboard scratched their faces. They heard the barking again. The noise stopped. The girls ran out of the creepy house and never spoke of it again... What was that?

Ella May (10)
Westfield Primary School, Radstock

THE HAUNTED HOUSE

James arrived outside the house. Slowly, he made his way to the front door. He knocked. Nothing. He knocked again. Nothing. It was now or never. It was here he had first spotted the horntail. He sat down and waited. In the end, he fell asleep on an aged sofa. He woke with a start. It was pitch-black. He picked up the only lantern. A vague outline darted at him. Running for his life, James looked for a way out. He closed a door behind him. *Bang!* The unknown crashed into the door. He jumped out a cracked window...

Chloe Porter (10)
Westfield Primary School, Radstock

THE CAMPING TRIP

Max was at a campsite for the weekend. Max wanted to see a pink elephant but he fell asleep waiting. Max woke up, bushes rustled. Something was out there! Unexpectedly, he found lots of fallen trees. He rushed to tell his parents but they were gone! Something crept up towards Max. What was it? Max got into the car and his parents came running in, not long after him.

In the end, they drove home, but little did they know that something was following them. It felt as if they should have never gone camping in the first place.

Jamie Cook (10)
Westfield Primary School, Radstock

THE OLD HOUSE

Suddenly, Luke heard a piercing scream from the top floor. He followed the echoes of little girls' and boys' screams. He made his way to the second floor. He looked for anything around him but nothing was up there. Luke started to sweat, he also began to worry. But then, some sort of noise came closer; the sound of a lullaby. Luke stayed as still as he possibly could because he knew now that something was in there as well. It was coming down the stairs... Luke hid from it then Luke ran. The doors opened and Luke ran home.

Oliver Filer (10)
Westfield Primary School, Radstock

JOE'S BIG ADVENTURE

Joe sat next to the river and watched as the kingfisher glided across the surface of the water. It was then she had first spotted the imps. All morning she waited until, in the end, her eyes closed and she slept, dreaming of majestic towers and spine-chilling castles and gnomes. It was only when she reached the road beyond the tree line that she stopped. She stood listening but only her heart thudded. It was as if the forest had swallowed its secret. "Imagine if I could get back in my house without my parents knowing..."

Adele Lansdown (11)
Westfield Primary School, Radstock

THE CURSE OF MARIGOLD COTTAGE

Max, James and Jacky were at Marigold Cottage to visit a friend, who had seen a magical creature. At the cottage, they went to the bedroom to wait for the creature, they fell asleep waiting.

Max woke up, it was night, he heard screaming. He investigated but saw nothing then he saw a red eye (like headlights) peering from the darkness. Despite being a careful person, he fell down the stairs. He was in a cold basement, where James and Jackie were tied up. Max freed them and took the clothes off that were on their faces and ran away.

Alfie Besser (11)
Westfield Primary School, Radstock

THE PECULIAR HOUSE!

School ended, Jasmine chatted to her friends whilst they walked home. She saw a weird house. Jasmine forgot her cup, she would have to run back and get it. But really she entered the house. It was old and creepy. Jasmine waited for the black cat to come that she saw walking. She fell asleep from waiting.

She heard a bang! Two red eyes peeped round the corner... so she ran! Her excitement with seeing the black cat gone, she ran till she reached the road beyond. She stopped. All she could hear was her heart thudding with pace. Silence.

Connie Raikes (11)
Westfield Primary School, Radstock

JOSH AND THE HAUNTED HOTEL

Josh woke up and went downstairs. He saw a track so he followed it. Josh made it to the end. There was a hotel. He sat in a room. Josh saw something. It was a baby T-rex. Then he fell asleep. Josh woke up. It was dark. He went back in the hotel. *Honk! Honk!* He heard something. "What was that?" Josh said. He heard a laugh. *Boom!* A red nose popped out of nowhere. He glimpsed a knife. Josh ran. He heard the knife being thrown. Josh cried. He was stabbed. *Poof!* "A dream! I'm alive! Yay, woohoo!"

Mason Faraday (10)
Westfield Primary School, Radstock

THE NIGHTMARE

Slowly Rosie left her room and strolled downstairs. Her pet monkey, Chimps, was waiting quietly. She slowly arrived after a long journey at a haunted cottage in Brazil. She put one step out of place and fell through a portal and she went somewhere… She went to an old prison in Germany. There was an old cell. She heard something behind her. It was a white figure standing in the distance. Rosie went to explore the prison. There was a seat and an old book. Creepy stuff started happening like stuff falling over her… But it was just a nightmare!

Caydence Ayling (11)
Westfield Primary School, Radstock

DERRICK AND THE SEA MONSTER!

Derrick crept downstairs, tiptoeing in case he got caught. Luckily, nobody was down there, so he left. Later, Derrick arrived at the beach. He loved it there. He stared weirdly at the water. At the beach he saw a big sea monster. It was humongous! Derrick heard a loud noise. He thought it might be the sea monster. Derrick was scared and tired. Derrick fell asleep.
When he woke up, he heard a loud noise. He was so anxious. Derrick went into the water to see what was making that loud noise. He thought the sea monster wouldn't come back...

Taylor James Willis (11)
Westfield Primary School, Radstock

THE MYSTERIOUS VISIT

Luke arrived at the house. The lawn was mown, there were flowers and the bushes were clipped. Luke knocked but there wasn't any answer. Luke sat down, watched the butterflies and waited. It was here he'd seen the phoenix. Luke yawned and leant back, asleep.
Luke woke and the grass had grown, the flowers had died and the house was damaged. Luke climbed in and looked around to see a shadow but it was not his grandma! The shadow darted and someone shouted, he turned to see someone. Luke bolted out the door, tripping over the steps and ran away.

Sennen Jeffery-Bradley (10)
Westfield Primary School, Radstock

THE LOCKED AWAY HOUSE

"Goodbye!" Megan said, sneaking home, which wasn't really home. Stealthily, she checked for any witnesses. Megan entered the house! It was really terrifying. She fell asleep after waiting hours for the cat. Suddenly she woke up with a start from a miaow, her clock had ticked 5:30. Hesitantly Megan crept after the cat, entering the house! The door slammed. Megan felt a heavy breath on the back of her neck. She didn't look! Megan spotted an empty hallway. She breathed in fresh air. Carefully she exhaled. Her secret had disappeared forever.

Olivia Swift (11)
Westfield Primary School, Radstock

THE CHASE IS ON!

Alone in the forest, Joe sat on a bench, as he watched the hornets eat pollen. It was here he first saw the fairy. He waited. Then, he started to feel drowsy and fell asleep, dreaming of elves and goblins.

He woke with a start, there were charred shadows, oily surfaces and wintry breezes. He pulled out a painful dart. Sticks snapped, leaves rustled and Joe got grabbed. Yellow eyes flickered, he ran. What was it? He couldn't see anything. Nothing! Feet thudding... At last, he was home. Little did he know, whatever it was, was waiting for him outside.

Chloe Cooper (10)
Westfield Primary School, Radstock

THE ABANDONED HOUSE

After walking for half an hour the children were tired and sat down in crunchy soft leaves and they waited. When they entered sinister woods they felt petrified! When they were running through the woods they came across an abandoned house and the door was wide open! The children walked through the door and they all fell over.

When they woke up, they all thought about what had happened even though they'd just got hit on the head. When they got upstairs they were frightened because they heard their names over and over again so they started to run out...

Louis Pride (10)
Westfield Primary School, Radstock

SPOOKY ADVENTURE

When she arrived at Rainbow Forest Isla saw butterflies flutter. Then she went to the spot where she first saw a unicorn. She waited for a while, but there was still no unicorn. Isla fell asleep while waiting, dreaming of a pink fluffy unicorn.

She woke up, the sun had slipped behind the trees. There was a vague silhouette, something moved towards her. *It's getting closer*, Isla thought. Suddenly there was a loud scream... She ran faster than she ever had before. When she reached the end of the forest, Isla walked home and never *ever* returned again...

Summer Grimes (10)
Westfield Primary School, Radstock

THE HUNTED SOMETHING IS COMING!

Ruby, Olivia and Lily got ready for a sleepover. Carefully, they went downstairs. Twenty minutes later, they were at Bethany's. She had a BBQ going, the girls went dashing in to eat. It started getting late, they played then went to bed. Thunder started. They woke up and went downstairs then stared into the darkness. Something moved... Someone touched Olivia, she screamed. A plate smashed on the floor. A scream echoed. They heard noises getting closer and louder! Someone tapped Olivia again, she screamed. But this time when the others turned around to see what was wrong... Olivia was gone!

Lataya Forde (10)
Westfield Primary School, Radstock

GRANDMA'S TOY MYSTERY

Maggie gazed out the shiny window for the rest of the journey to Grandma's. At her grandma's, she charged to the attic. Waiting for her toys she scanned the butterflies on the roof. Slowly, she slept, dreaming of her grandma and the toys.

Later, she woke up looking for the toys. Then the butterflies disappeared. Something had fallen. An ebony creature with red eyes slowly came forward. She stared at it, horrified, then she tripped over something and crawled out the room. At the bottom, the toys appeared but one was missing. A sharp hiss came from upstairs...

"What's that?"

Leilah Jones (10)
Westfield Primary School, Radstock

THE BREATH

Silently, Amanda poked her head around the door. Gently she crept downstairs. She could hear snoring. Carefully, she opened a door. Eventually, she reached a dungeon. Dust everywhere... Nothing... Lampshades flickered quickly. She fell asleep on a Victorian armchair. Amanda woke with a start. Everything was more ominous. Soon after she felt a warm breath on her neck. A shudder went down her spine. She sprinted speedily. Cautiously she opened the door just enough to fit through. The spiderweb-infested staircase was dark. As she got to the top she realised the door was wide open... Her heart thudded...

Mya-May Waldron (10)
Westfield Primary School, Radstock

HANGMAN'S CAVE

Slowly, Dwayne crept downstairs. He scanned for witnesses. He finally got to the door. His dog wanted to play.

Later, he arrived at Hangman's Cave. He leapt inside and searched around the place fearlessly. He fell asleep. Soon after, he woke up. The place was now disgusting. He heard a terrifying shriek. He tiptoed through it. A clear silhouette darted! Dwayne received goosebumps and heard a blood-curdling scream. He ran like a cheetah. He cut himself harshly on the rocks. Something breathed... He leapt into the reeds. He was out of dreadful Hangman's Cave. He heard again something breathing...

John Saunders (10)
Westfield Primary School, Radstock

THE TRIP TO THE SOUTH POLE

Once a boy asked his dad to go to the South Pole. The boy's name was Richy Rich, he flew to the South Pole. When he arrived an elf took him to his room, Richy heard a thud. He ran downstairs and he saw Evil Santa.
Evil Santa tied Richy up and made him a slave. Evil Santa pointed a laser at Richy, then there was a crash. Uncle Elliot came to save Richy. Elliot fought Evil Santa. Elliot untied Richy and they flew back to America where they lived happily ever after.

Rhys Murphy (11)
VLC Primary School, Milton

THE STORM

In a cold, damp room, a little boy woke up and saw a dark figure. The thunder outside sounded like a plane crashing and the lightning flashed like headlights. Breathing heavily and feeling hot like he was in an oven, the little boy tried to hide but he was so frightened, he felt like he was paralysed. The figure started getting closer and closer. He closed his eyes, then the bedroom light switched on. He slowly opened his eyes and was relieved to see his brother in front of him.

James Pearce (10)
VLC Primary School, Milton

FOREST HUNTER

Deep in the depths of the forest, there was a boy. He was haunting a poltergeist. The problem was that the poltergeist was haunting him too but he didn't know! Every time the boy took a step the poltergeist wanted to say hi but he was too scared so he followed quickly behind him instead.

As he walked the boy heard a creak behind him. "H-hello?" he stammered nervously. "Will you be my friend?" asked the poltergeist. Even though he was scared he said, "Okay," because who knows what would have happened otherwise.

Kyros Alabaf (9)
VLC Primary School, Milton

NEW HOME

One day, there was a boy that was alone. He woke up in horror in a spooky corridor full of shadows. He shot up, screaming, "Help, ghosts everywhere!"
A man appeared, covered in blood and crept towards him... "Come with me little boy," he whispered then the man disappeared into the blackness.
The boy asked, "Which way is the way out?" in a worried voice.
The old man hobbled back, holding the hand of a boy in pyjamas. "My name is Jack. This is not a dream," said the boy in the pyjamas. "This is your new home little boy."

Rhys Jefferies (10)
VLC Primary School, Milton

BLOOD NIGHT

I saw the full moonlit sky over the graveyard. I had an idea to murder Isabelle, the person who put me in the grave. Next to me was a tower where Isabelle was but first I had to brutally torture and kill her mum. I then walked to my dog's grave, I was sad that I was the only one alive. I had to kill them all; Mum, Dad and her cat. I ran to the tower. I killed her family now, not her. I walked to her and stabbed her twice. Dead. Bloodbath.

Will Murphy (9)
St Georges Church School, St Georges

THE MONSTER UNDER THE BED

Thud! Bobby woke up with a start and hit his head on the ceiling. When he came back to his senses he realised a noise had come from underneath his bed. He looked under the bed and he saw it! It was the weirdest thing he'd ever seen. Then he ran into the library. When he got there he found the book of monsters but he couldn't find anything like the monster so he went back to his room and looked under his bed and found his dog there!

Jack Knight (10)
St Georges Church School, St Georges

BLOOD OF THE DEAD

I woke up in a hall of cells. I was alone, or was I? In the distance, I heard a deep scream like a zombie. I saw a stooped figure running towards me so I grabbed my shotgun and killed it. Then a huge horde of zombies came after me, so I ran to the roof. There was a machine there so I put my gun in it and the machine upgraded it. I fought the horde but then a heavily armoured zombie came running after me and we had a vicious fight. Finally I killed it and won!

Oscar Povey (10)
St Georges Church School, St Georges

THE HAUNTED MANSION

In the woods there was a mansion, it was haunted. As I walked in the forest, I saw it. It looked like an abandoned mansion from the old days. It was big and scary. I didn't like it. Inside, the door slammed shut on me. A shadow followed me. I heard a laugh. It sounded like a clown laughing. I saw a red balloon with blood on it. I walked into the room and saw an open window but when I got out, the clown chased me away. It was scary and I didn't like it.

Oliver Lock (9)
St Georges Church School, St Georges

THE DEATH OF JIM

When I left my house, I noticed a very strange house, it looked like it was a haunted house. I went in and shouted, "Hello?" Nobody answered. I slowly walked into the house. As I walked in, I noticed traps on the floor and a skeleton ahead caught in a trap. I walked further into the house. When I got to the end of the hall, I saw an old man watching TV. He bellowed, "Run for your life!" I ran and ran but I stepped on the trap. *Snap!* I died.

Joshua Kirby (9)
St Georges Church School, St Georges

THE DEATH OF LITTLE GIRLS

On a pitch-black night, some little girls went trick or treating. They had so much candy. When they heard whispering voices coming from the distance all of the girls thought it would be funny to trick or treat on a prison. When they got to the prison they pounded with all their might and the door just opened randomly and they got yanked in by someone inside. It was dark. They were running down an aisle and suddenly they all died. It was a mystery who killed them all at once. Who did it?

Spencer Craig (9)
St Georges Church School, St Georges

THE HORRIFYING FOREST! BEWARE NOT TO FRIGHT!

On a blood-curdling night, a girl slept in a mysterious forest. The girl had wavy hair and bulging blue eyes. Her name was Olivia. As she woke up she realised she was in the one and only Haunted Forest! She climbed the tree and then she started to see lots of animals but they were not cute little animals, they were hypnotised animals. In the distance she saw a monkey and she climbed higher. She heard a gun and, oh no, the monkey came and saw her then... *Bang!* She was on the floor!

Saphie-Mae Johnstone (10)
St Georges Church School, St Georges

THE CREEPY GRAVEYARD

Once in a creepy, misty graveyard, there were three kids who went trick or treating. They thought it was funny to go in the graveyard but then the misty floor shook. Someone came to life, she was called Isabella. The kids were horrified and they screamed. She needed a potion and she asked the kids to help her. They all made a potion out of leaves and tried it, it didn't work. They made it again, this time it worked! And before returning to the dead, she gave the kids a good luck potion.

Izzy Hawley (9)
St Georges Church School, St Georges

THE HAUNTED HOSPITAL

It was at a haunted hospital that a person called Jake was exploring. There was stuff thrown around the gigantic hospital. He heard a cup smash. Then there was whispering. "Hello, hello..." with a high-pitched voice. Jake started to search to find out where it came from. He found an underground basement. He found a mirror. He went into it. He went and looked into it and saw a ghost behind him. He turned around and this time saw nothing. After a while, he left the hospital to go home.

Henry Zajac (9)
St Georges Church School, St Georges

THE BOY AND THE DEMON

He woke up gasping for air, his book fell off the shelf. He stood up carefully and walked to his bedroom wall and opened the door. Cold went up his spine. He went back to his room and lit some candles, he wished for whoever was scaring him to leave. He heard a devilish voice saying, "Never!"

He lit 12 candles. He got out a special rock to keep him safe and stood still and said, "God take him back."

It went silent... He got up and ran back to bed and hid under his quilt.

Oliver Beer (11)
St Georges Church School, St Georges

BANNED

Banned from school, I ran up the hill. Upset, I hadn't done anything! I couldn't face Mum, I just couldn't. She would be furious at me. By the time I got to the top of the hill it was midnight. My phone had rung about six times. Mum was worried. I looked around; overgrown plants were clinging to the house and scratching came from inside. The moon shone down to a gravestone as if it was showing me the way. I stared at it... I read it: 'Joe Kins...' That's me! What did that mean?

Emma Louise Payne (10)
St Georges Church School, St Georges

THE VALENTINE'S NOTE

I was at work and someone had left a Valentine's note for me on my desk. I didn't think much about it. I got home and opened it straight away but I was confused, it wasn't a Valentine's note, it said: 'To Imogen. Roses are red, violets are blue, I killed your family and I'm gonna kill you. Go to the bathroom'.
I ran to the bathroom and found my family hanging from the ceiling; dead, and in a gap between them another note was hanging. It said: 'Reserved for Imogen'.

Imogen Harris (10)
St Georges Church School, St Georges

THE NIGHT BEFORE THE SPOOKY MONSTER APPEARED

It was the night before Halloween. A little boy thought Halloween was tonight so he went to knock on a haunted house's door. It slightly opened so he stepped in and the door slammed shut. He heard a bang and shouted, "Who is there?"
He heard a ghost go, "Whoo!" He then ran after him and caught him with a net and threw the ghost around. He laid there without moving and then he suddenly turned into a boy and then back into a ghost again. The boy was too frightened so he went back home.

Skarlett Wickens (10)
St Georges Church School, St Georges

HAUNTED DOLL

On the darkest night of all, Georgia and Esme went to the park. On the way, they saw a haunted house so they decided to go in. The door slammed shut behind them. It was all dark and creepy. Georgia and Esme found a door that said: *Beware! Don't come in. Danger!* They ran down a corridor and found that the doors slammed shut. They were trapped. They went out of a room and there was a doll behind them with a knife in its hand. "Argh!" shouted Georgia and Esme. What happened next? Were they okay?

Jorja Wickens (10)
St Georges Church School, St Georges

SHADOWS

Ghost saw Ella coming home and he rushed to the door to get to her. Ella was walking to the door and noticed something strange and very peculiar; a black figure was standing behind the bush. Ella moved over to the bush but she felt dizzy and crashed to the ground. Ghost was horrified.
She woke up in an attic. Ghost made his way into the hallway but went to Ella's room. He was too scared. All Ghost heard was a mutter then a blood-curdling scream. The figure was Raven, he had killed several people in this house.

Izabella Hoskin-Love (9)
St Georges Church School, St Georges

TERROR IN THE HOUSE

On a dark and spine-chilling night, Rebecca and her family were going trick or treating but they had recently moved house so they were going somewhere new. They were going down their lane when they came to a haunted house. Rebecca's family wanted to go inside but Rebecca disagreed.

After half an hour she just went in. When they went in they went down to the basement. There was a blood-curdling monster with a gun. *Bang!* In a flash Rebecca and her family were on the floor, dead! They were never seen again.

Issy Josie Lanning (10)
St Georges Church School, St Georges

A MOUSE FROM A HAUNTED HOUSE

It was a spooky morning, my face lit up as a witch was standing, creating a potion to fix her horrible nose. From my hole, I watched the witch make herself a cheese sandwich. My eyes met her and I ran like a rocket towards the table, leapt on the bin and launched myself onto her arm. "Argh!" She whipped me into her potion. I swam for a while yet her blood-curdling grin made me sink. Once I awoke, my new fangs tingled, my bloodshot eyes saw the witch. Then I had a sudden thirst for blood... "Argh!"

Isla Connolly (11)
St Georges Church School, St Georges

THE HAUNTED HOUSE

On the gloomiest night of all a boy named Tom went into a house he found in an abandoned woods. That house was haunted. He went inside and *creak!* went the door as he walked in. There was mess everywhere and cracked windows. Tom went upstairs and saw at least one thousand dead bodies. Little did he know he soon would be one. Tom saw a wardrobe and he opened it. "Argh!" he screamed. There was something inside. It was a clown. "Please don't kill me!" shouted Tom, but those were his last words.

Katie Pinner (9)
St Georges Church School, St Georges

THE HOTEL CLOWN

"Mum!" shouted Vicky and Natalie. They had lost her in the hotel in Spain where they were staying. It was Halloween and the children who were ten years old couldn't find their mum anywhere. They walked down a dark corridor where a black and white clown jumped out, scaring them. He had a blue and white knife. The girls screamed and Mum came running down the corridor. The girls were scared, they had seen a clown but were happy to find their mum. The clown took off his mask, but it was just their mum's friend!

Ariana Hamlin (9)
St Georges Church School, St Georges

THE MOVING HOUSE

On a spine-chilling night, in a street called Misty-Inn, there was a girl called Lucie, she was known to go trick or treating every day. So one night she walked up to an abandoned house. Well, she thought it was abandoned. She rang the doorbell, she was terrified because she didn't know if anyone would answer or not. Suddenly, someone answered and dragged her in. She saw dolls moving on their own, whispering voices and some sweets going into her basket. But then she realised it was supposed to be scary, it was Halloween.

Faith Murray (9)
St Georges Church School, St Georges

OLLIE THE VAMPIRE

Ollie the vampire was in the garage drinking a cup of blood. Suddenly the door slammed and the light turned off but the worst thing was there was blood all over the floor. "Hello, is anyone there?" Then Ollie bumped into a huge boy who was a ghost. "I hope you're not coming to kill me."
He had a rope in his hand, he tied me up and he threw me in the messiest place in the garage. The worst thing was I was lying in the blood, and screaming for help. "You'll never get out of here!" he screamed.

Julia Stankiewicz (9)
St Georges Church School, St Georges

THE HEADLESS GHOST

On a dark and stormy night, a dog barked in fear. A young boy chased after him, stumbling over twigs and rocks in what he thought was a forest. They reached a clearing and found a haunted house. A strange noise echoed through the forest. Provoked, the boy's dog ran through the open door. The boy followed him, shouting, "Rex! Rex!" There was no reply. Suddenly a chill ran through his spine. A ghost carried his own head! The boy ran for his life, through corridors, up a rickety old ladder, which led to an attic. He was cornered...

Tamsen Markham (10)
St Georges Church School, St Georges

THE DEATH OF MILLIE

It was the night of Halloween when Millie died. Here's how... Millie was really excited to get many sweets as it was Halloween night. This year she was allowed to go out by herself. It was beginning to darken when she got to a weird house. She went in. It was alright for the first minute, then Millie heard a voice saying, "Look behind you, I can see you!"
Millie wanted to scream but nothing came out. The voice stopped. After five seconds a creepy doll started to crawl towards her with a knife and, *pow!* The doll killed her.

Maddison Hughes (9)
St Georges Church School, St Georges

BLACK MIST

In the darkest part of the forest there was nothing but the corpse of the mailman. Twenty-four hours earlier, the mailman (Jim) knocked on the door of an abandoned house. The door opened itself and welcomed him in. Suddenly, he noticed a dark mist rising up. Jim heard the call of an old man, "Help!" he screamed. Jim's feet started to sprint forward to the man. There was nobody there. The scream of the old man could still be heard by Jim. He turned around only to find a black figure with lava-red eyes. A spine-chilling feeling filled him...

Max Cooper (10)
St Georges Church School, St Georges

MYSTERY MURDER

One moonlit night, two werewolves were going hunting for food. Their names were Zen (the boy) and Zodiac (the alpha female), they were brother and sister. When they reached the abandoned campsite, Zen said to Zodiac, "You go and hunt for some meat, I will stay in case a fluffy little rabbit comes."
So Zen stayed at the campsite but was scared in case something happened to him. A few minutes later (felt like hours), Zodiac came back with a fat duck and juicy deer, as she turned around to share the food she saw Zen was lying motionless. Dead...

Paige Richardson (10)
St Georges Church School, St Georges

STRANGE NOISES IN THE ATTIC

Creak! went the attic door. Something or someone was in there. Madeline decided to go in to explore. She opened the attic door and dead bodies fell all on her head. It was horrifying. While she was up there Madeline heard strange noises coming closer to her so she hid behind a small box. She tried to run to the opening of the attic but someone was guarding it. There was a ghost. The ghost could see things from far away and he floated behind her. Suddenly, "Argh!" screamed Madeline. What happened? Was she okay? What's going to happen next?

Gabi Niec (9)
St Georges Church School, St Georges

THE GRAVEYARD HOUSE

On a gruesome night in the graveyard, Fanta went out to play. Then he saw Shadow with blood around his mouth. That night, Fanta went to sleep thinking about what he had seen. And then, Shadow stood at the end of his bed, blood dripping on the floor. Fanta hoped it was a dream but he knew it wasn't. As the monster crept closer, Fanta screamed, "Argh!" then his father, Grampta, came in the room.
Shadow freaked and returned to his place in the graveyard by his spine-chilling master's coffin, at the end of the field near the vampire's lair.

Gethin Williams (10)
St Georges Church School, St Georges

THE MASSIVE SCARE

On a horrifying, spooky night I was in my attic getting ready for Halloween but when I came back upstairs from the bathroom, there were objects moving around and jumping. My bowl of make-up wouldn't stop moving around, I couldn't get them! Finally, I had my make-up to get ready.

So, after two hours I was ready. I went trick or treating on hidden houses and when I came back I had my sweets in the attic to make sure no one got them. Then a massive spider jumped out. An eyeball popped out. "We've found you!" it said.

"Argh!"

Roxsi Wakzak (9)
St Georges Church School, St Georges

ENTITY

On a silent, wild night, Kevin heard groaning and blood-curdling screams from an old toilet factory. The last words he heard were, "Ho... Argh!" He froze in fear. He heard the door swinging open but no one was there. Suddenly, he saw his sister with no eyes! There was blood pouring out of her eyeholes. Then a tall dark figure stabbed Kevin's sister. Kevin pulled out a sword and swung it at him but it went right through him. Kevin heard something behind him and... slashed Kevin's head clean off. Who caused this tragedy to happen? Who was the murderer?

Charlie Baxter-James (9)
St Georges Church School, St Georges

THE DEATH OF MADDISON, THAT'S A DOLL!

One dark, gloomy night, Maddison was asleep in a haunted house. Every night at 3am/Devil's Hour she would wake up and hear the sound of laughter in the attic. A creepy gang of zombies were dancing around the gloomy house. Suddenly she found the zombies! She was terrified.
Five minutes later, "Argh!" she shouted. "Help!" The zombies fought her. Later she had one more zombie to defeat but it was the gold one. She had a gun somewhere in her house. She shot the zombie. Suddenly she ran out of ammo then the zombie killed her wearing noob skin.

Maddison Mansfield (9)
St Georges Church School, St Georges

GO TO SLEEP

It was my friend, Jay's, curiosity that brought us to this abandoned mental asylum. At first, everything was okay, besides the constant urge to leave. After endless minutes of exploring each dimly lit and dirty hall, we agreed on leaving. I turned around, only to be instantly stopped by the blood-curdling scream of my friend. My gaze averted back to him, making my eyes widen. Jay was being dragged away. Before I could reach, the lights flickered and went out. A cold hand clasped over my mouth, muffling my shouts for help. "Go to sleep..." was all I could hear.

Poppy Siviter (11)
St Georges Church School, St Georges

THE TRANSPARENT FIGURE

On a dark and gloomy night on Halloween, an eleven-year-old boy was out at 8.10pm knocking on people's doors. He was the only person out where he was. There were spooky noises and he kept seeing things. Were they following him? He didn't know. Behind him, he heard, "I'm following you!"
As Racurly turned around a transparent figure was staring him in the eyes. "Argh!" Racurly ran all the way home where he hid under his duvet. There were then noises under his bed. All of a sudden a skeleton jumped out from under his bed. "Oh my!"

Keira Lovell (10)
St Georges Church School, St Georges

THE VINDA VIPER

There lived two boys on a rainy night, Bob and Jimmy. Bob was brave, Jimmy was alarmed. There was a haunted mansion. Jimmy dared Bob to prove he was brave by going into the haunted mansion for twenty minutes. When he got there, he froze, listening to the deafening phone. He answered, scared, it said, "I am the Vinda Viper, I'll be there in 20 minutes!"
His spine tingled weirdly. Twenty minutes later, he opened the door anxiously.
He said, "I am the Vinda Viper!"
Bob ran home, breathing quickly until he got to this warm, cosy, sweet bed.

Bradley Alexander Reynolds (10)
St Georges Church School, St Georges

MURDER HOUSE

On a blood-curdling night, two twins threw a massive rave after they graduated university. The appearance of a boy was quite queer and made Jenny freeze. Jenny yelled, "Did you invite him?"
While Jenny waited for a reply she went to get some fresh air. Kenny went to the kitchen and saw a dead boy on the floor but before he could check he was just playing around, *slice!*
Jenny sprinted but before she got to the door...
"Wake up!" yelled their mother.
"Woah! What just happened?" whispered Jenny.
Suddenly Kenny woke up and yelled...

Ellie Hawley (11)
St Georges Church School, St Georges

THE SCREAM STREET!

"Boo!" shouted Gingy.
Bones got scared, he fell apart and Willy fell from the roof because he was sleeping.
Suddenly the doorbell rang. Gingy went to answer it and it was a huge, scary monster. "Roar!"
"Argh!" screamed Gingy. "Run!"
They all climbed out the back door but the monster could see over the top of the house so he followed them and crushed their house. It was not the first time he'd done that. The monster had a sword and he tried swinging at them but he hit a lamp post and hit himself on the head. "Argh!"

Ashton Gilmore (11)
St Georges Church School, St Georges

THE DEATH

In the abandoned basement, Chloe was hiding. She was playing hide-and-seek with her little brother. Three hours later, Josh ran in and kicked the door open. He was holding a gun. He sang a song... "Come out, come out wherever you are!"
Chloe screamed in terror. Josh laughed, "Hahaha, it's only fake!"
Two hours later, dinner. There was a knock on the door and crackling. It was Josh the jack-o'-lantern. "Do you know Chloe Blackwell?" Mum replied, "Umm, yes, she's eating dinner." Chloe ran out into the basement and hid again.

Nicola Walczak (11)
St Georges Church School, St Georges

THE NEW YORK TERROR

Last year, in an old factory in the dangerous city of New York, there was a scary man called Laserbeam, who had killed twenty-four people and robbed ten more! He'd stolen stuff from shops like guns and cigars, also matches and money! He'd stolen five cars! He'd kidnapped forty kids and ten adults. He'd robbed four houses.

Laserbeam was on top of the Brooklyn Bridge, going towards the factory, with a gun in his hand. When he got in the factory he heard some teenagers talking so Laserbeam shot twenty. Police and ambulances came. The police shot. *Bang!* Laserbeam died.

Riley Winfield (10)
St Georges Church School, St Georges

A NIGHT IN THE HOSPITAL

"Argh!" One moonlit, apocalyptic night, three boys crept out of bed. They all met up at the central park. Their names were Zack, James and Edward. They travelled to an abandoned hospital where they found tables and even cups of stale coffee. All of a sudden, they heard a sound behind them. "Ergh!"
They all shrieked out, "Zombie!" and they ran through the corridors like there was no tomorrow. Out of every door, more and more zombies came rushing out. "Argh!"
Edward fell down. *Bash!* Another zombie jumped out on James. Another gruesome zombie jumped on Zack. "Argh!"

Jack Edward Weetch (10)
St Georges Church School, St Georges

TRUTH OR DARE?

On a dark, stormy night, a girl called Amie went out trick or treating. *Creak!* A door opened as soon as she walked in. *Slam!* It slammed closed. "La la la la..." sung a creepy doll. The doll said, "Truth or dare?"
Amie replied, "Um, truth."
The doll demanded Amie say 'dare'.
"No!" shouted Amie.
"Yes!" shouted the doll.
"Why?" said Amie. "Why do you want me to say 'dare'?"
"Because I've been dared to, so, truth or dare?"
"Dare!" yelled Amie.
Pow! Amie vanished.

Amie March (10)
St Georges Church School, St Georges

CREAK!

On a blood-curdling night, John and Billy were going to a teenager's party. Billy whispered to John, "I don't feel confident about this night." John whispered back, "Everything is going to be alright." So they carried on with the night, kinda speedwalking to the party now.
Suddenly they made it, but John noticed there was a creepy, glowing haunted house. Billy, sounding like he had a frog in his throat said, "We're not going in there are we?"
John replied, "Damn straight we are!"
Billy noticed all the smashed windows and everything. Suddenly they heard... *creak!*

Harry Watts (11)
St Georges Church School, St Georges

THE BASEMENT

In his new house, Dylan was awake in bed. He couldn't get to sleep. So he decided to go exploring. His parents told him to never go into the basement so he thought he would start there. Once he was on the first step he could hear lots of noises. Suddenly something tripped him up and he was sent tumbling down. Quickly he got to his feet and looked around.
"Argh! Who's there?" asked Dylan, scared to death.
"I'm Spooky and I need a friend."
"I'll be your friend."
"Let's play a game."
"Okay, what game?"
"Lunchtime."
"Okay."
Chomp!

Dylan Welch (10)
St Georges Church School, St Georges

ARE GHOSTS REAL?

It was a cold winter's evening and Isaac, Max and Tamsin were making their way to Hillsbrough, which was a nearby village. Apparently, Hillsbrough's haunted but they didn't believe that. They thought zombies, mummies and ghosts were a pile of rubbish, but boy were they wrong. Soon enough, they arrived and made their way to the door of a haunted house. "Let's go inside!"
They walked in, hearts struck with fear. Whilst walking upstairs, a ghostly, misty figure appeared out of the darkness. "So you still think ghosts aren't real?"
"Run!" they screamed. Mummies and ghosts surrounded them... *"Aaaaaahhh!"*

Matthew Ncube (10)
St Georges Church School, St Georges

THE HAUNTED GRAVEYARD

On Halloween night, the forests shook while people were trick or treating at houses. At the local graveyard, a mum and her two children were watering the flowers and trees until, *howl, howl!* "Argh!" the children screamed.
"It's okay, Mum's here to protect you," Maria mumbled.
Howl, howl! The monster edged closer until Maria noticed. "That's not a monster, it's Recket and Ralph doing tricks!"
The children sprinted towards the puppies in relief. *Crackle! Crackle!* The ground shook.
"Argh! Not again!" the children screeched.
But who knows if the monsters were real. *Howl! Roar! Stomp! Creak! Howl!*

Carys Welch (9)
St Georges Church School, St Georges

THE MYSTERIOUS GIRL

I jumped into the car and I saw something very strange; a little girl was staring at me. She had a white face with straight hair. I blinked. She was gone. At school I saw her outside, I wondered if anyone could see her but, no. I saw her all week. On Friday, we had school photos. All weekend I didn't see her. I got my school photos on Monday and took them home. I showed my family and we were all terrified. The girl I kept seeing was standing next to me in the photo for all to see.

Laura Shaw (9)
North Newton Community Primary School, North Newton

MY NIGHTMARES

I shiver in the corner of the room, nails are stuck in the walls, dust falls from the ceiling; I choke to death. My breathing follows a ball of light. Is it a ghost? Soon enough, the ball moves out through my locked door. My gaze moves to a ruby-red eye. It's a vampire. I turn to run, but a wall is there to stop me. The vampire flies out of the window. Suddenly, a portrait moves. It stares straight at me. I wake up, it's just a dream. I'm in my bed under the covers and safe.

Lily Grindrod (9)
North Newton Community Primary School, North Newton

THE PUPPET

I woke up, I wasn't at home. "Mummy, Daddy?" I shouted. There was no answer. Suddenly a puppet was tearing at me. The puppy said his name was Slappy without hesitation. The puppet spoke again. "Your mummy and daddy are dead," he shouted. The door crept open. It was a werewolf, blood was dripping out of his mouth; they both went out of the room. The oven turned on, there was a body in the oven. I opened it up, it was made out of wax. It was a trick. Slappy had a knife...

Jayjay Hancock (9)
North Newton Community Primary School, North Newton

HIM

I just moved into a new house and at my doorstep were twins, they said he was buried just down the dark, gloomy road then ran away. Since I was so curious, I walked there step by step. I arrived at what seemed like an abandoned church. I could hear crying. "It was him who abandoned me!" I crept inside to see a white spirited figure. "You, it was you," wept the woman. I sped out panting, through the corner of my eye I saw a tomb with my name on it, my birthday and today I'm him.

Brandon Burton (10)
North Newton Community Primary School, North Newton

THE SHED

What is that thing? A broken, slanted shed at the end of the garden, scratched like a ravenous bear tore it open. I crept towards it, with the sound of squelching mud on my shoes. As I got closer... I blinked. It moved. I don't know how, but it did! Within arm's reach, loud thuds could be heard like a heart beating. The door creaked. I feared the worst, I appeared in a run-down train yard. I noticed someone lurking in the darkness. I ran. I ran to a dead end with nowhere to go. I turned around...

Raiin Walker (11)
North Newton Community Primary School, North Newton

THE SPOOKY ROOM

Carefully opening the door, I felt a shiver down my spine. It tickled. The door was open, in the top corner there was a bunch of spiders. "Argh!" A spider just dropped in front of me. In the drawers, there were snakes and crabs. Under the bed there were zombies. I screamed as loudly as I could, but no one came. Not even my mum and not my hero dad. Terrified, I ran for the exit but it was blocked by snakes and spiders. Finally I got out of my room. My heart was beating so fast. Never ever again!

Freya Bult (9)
North Newton Community Primary School, North Newton

TRAPPED

A pitch-black room, I looked at my surroundings but saw a blood-covered cloth lying next to the blood-coated saw. I moved closer. A hand grabbed my face and pulled me into a hole. I resisted and flung myself backwards and smashed some glass. I turned... Spiders - millions of them. I ran for the door. I shook it, it didn't open. Now I knew there was no escape! "Help me!" I screamed for help at the top of my lungs. No one replied. It was hopeless. I sat down, waiting for death to capture my soul.

Sonny Morris (11)
North Newton Community Primary School, North Newton

NIGHTMARES COME TRUE

I woke up in the night to a loud rumble in my room. I felt something under my bed. The room was darker than the night sky. The deafening, desperate cries of my heart and the sound of my creaky wooden floor were getting louder and louder. The sounds of demonic terror, trauma and deathly hate were coming to my door. I crept out of my darkness-filled den half expecting to see my dad in his blue dressing gown, but what actually came was beyond imagination. A demon from the dark stared at me. It launched itself at me...

Jakob Jones (10)
North Newton Community Primary School, North Newton

MONSTER MANSION

I knew I shouldn't have been there, but I was so curious. The abandoned house on the hill looked sinister and haunting. It was a moonlit night when I opened the door. I felt a shiver go down my spine. I heard bells jingling somewhere in the house. I froze, heart pounding, palms sweating. A monster's mouth opened, it was so big I could see the back of his throat. "Have you come for tea?" he asked coldly. I looked up and the hideous, slimy monster had appeared in front of me. It had an enormous grin on its face...

Callum Little (10)
North Newton Community Primary School, North Newton

MY SPOOKY ADVENTURE

I finally got to the end of the corridor in the spooky house. Where was I? I was in a small room. The plain wallpaper was peeling off. The dusty wooden wardrobe hadn't been opened in years. Where was the way out? Scared, frightened, worried. I heard a noise from behind me. "Is anyone there?" I turned around slowly to see a tall, dark figure standing above me. I screamed. I was shaking with fear. I stood still for a moment to find my voice again and then the light went on.
"Boo!" It was only Dad checking on me.

Libby Quinn (10)
North Newton Community Primary School, North Newton

MYSTERY MANSION

It was 12pm, I had just knocked on Mrs Bustleworth's door in my skeleton costume for some candy. Suddenly, in the corner of my eye, I spotted a colossal dark and terror-filling spooky mansion. As I slowly crept towards the barricaded building, I believe I glimpsed a gloomy, misty shadow through the dusty glass. Furthermore, I leapt onto the porch. Terrified, with a shaking hand, I leaned out for the doorbell, I pressed it once, once again and ag... I was met face-to-face with the most spine-shaking, fear-filling scary being in my life...

James Griffiths (11)
North Newton Community Primary School, North Newton

THE WORST NIGHT

I heard sounds coming from under my bed, I wondered what they were. They were clitter-clattering, like swords banging against each other. I rose from my bed and thought what possibly it could be until it pulled me under my bed... It was a non-skinned, bony figure with black, gloomy eyes. Underneath my bed was coated with cobwebs and large, matt-black spiders crawling up and down, along my walls and even in my bed! I'm pretty sure I also saw a tarantula too! "Argh!" Everything from under my bed was on me. I suddenly awoke with great confusion.

Grace Palmer (11)
North Newton Community Primary School, North Newton

WHAT COULD I BE?

I lay in my bed trying to sleep. Everything was silent except my alarm clock, which was ticking away. It had just struck midnight. I sat up, the crooked door creaked, I looked closer. Some kind of creature moved swiftly towards me, it looked like blood was falling out of its eyes and crawling down its cheeks. Suddenly, a shadow washed over me. It was like a wave. What was I thinking? Scared, worried, frightened. I yelled for help and I dived under my bed. Surprisingly, both my mum and dad came frantically running in. "Argh!" I yelled. "Help me!"

Lola Whatley (10)
North Newton Community Primary School, North Newton

THE APPROACHING DEATH!

"Mama, Mama!" I woke up quivering, as I heard crying. Looking around, there was nothing until... I saw it; my doll glaring threateningly back at me. As an ear-piercing scream lingered, I turned to see more, screaming, crying, whimpering, laughing. The night grew darker as lightning pierced the gloomy grey sky. Shadows and silhouettes danced around my bed, as a menacing smile sent shivers up my spine. Goosebumps travelled along my arms, while I tried to escape. Nowhere to run, nowhere to hide. I screamed for help, but no one heard me. She launched rapidly at me...

Faye Little (11)
North Newton Community Primary School, North Newton

THE SCARIEST DAY OF MY LIFE

Quickly I ran through the park, I tripped, then I was falling. "Where am I?" Suddenly I could feel something lurking behind me, I glimpsed a shadow. An old rag doll was staring at me! Did she move? "Who's there?"
A voice deep and husky boomed, "I'm the spirit of the cellar!"
I could feel a presence rushing around me like a tornado ready to destroy. I tried to move but couldn't, something was controlling me, but how? Ten ghosts suddenly appeared but they looked like the doll, maybe they were... "What are you?" I yelled, trying to run away...

Sophie Bult (10)
North Newton Community Primary School, North Newton

SOMETHING POSSESSED

"Mum? Dad?" The door was still shut. A rattle came from under the bed. I was petrified. Cautiously, I looked. "Three, two, one..." My eyes closed unintentionally. I tried to open them but it was impossible, it was like something was possessing me. That thing definitely didn't want to show their appearance. The curtains (that hid the moon from anyone's vision) were knocked off by something revealing the unbearable, frightening and brisk lightning attacks. I hid under my bed. Cold wind gusted on the back of my neck. I turned around and spotted two red eyes glaring into my soul...

Richard Robertson (11)
North Newton Community Primary School, North Newton

HAUNTED HALLOWEEN

Scared, confused and horrified, I hid under my bed, outside was a zombie apocalypse. It wasn't just zombies though; scary skeletons and spooky werewolves rang at the door. I covered my face, the whole world was drifting. My worst nightmares had come true, I was terrified. Frankenstein, witches and evil puppets/dolls lurked outside. Even Snickers, my favourite chocolates were there. Suddenly I remembered my child's monster repellent so I ran upstairs and got it. Blood drizzled from my wife's mouth. I locked her in a cupboard. I was scared, scared for my life. The front door opened. "Trick or treat?"

Benjamin Murray (10)
North Newton Community Primary School, North Newton

ABBY'S SPOOKY ADVENTURE

In a forbidden graveyard, with mossy RIP stones, there lay a monster of the dead. At 3am when the moon shone on the graveyard, Abby entered the place of doom. Suddenly the mysterious, mischievous monster rose from their sleepy slumber whilst the creaky, rusty gates opened by themselves. *Creak! Creak!* "What/who are you?" Abby questioned with fear.
A tall, dark figure lurked around Abby. The figure with sharp, pointed claws grasped Abby by her legs and swung her around and around. Abby yelled, "Help! Help!" but no one answered. Abby wasn't seen again, it's still a mystery to this day.

Olivia Contreras (9)
North Newton Community Primary School, North Newton

FRIGHT NIGHT

One autumn night, two boisterous, excited boys were setting off to a party. Cycling down a dark, dreary street, they passed freaky-faced pumpkins, sinister skeletons and grotesque ghosts all ready for the spookiest time of year. "Argh!" screamed the boys and laughed as it was just a werewolf on a wall. The rain cascaded out of the pumpkins' mouths. There were terrifying tarantulas on gates and vampires on windows... Slime was trickling down the handle and as they approached the hall, "Boo."
"Eek, it sure is the school Halloween disco." They entered the horrifying hall. Fright Night was awaiting them.

Jamie Gauld (10)
North Newton Community Primary School, North Newton

MUM, DAD

One dark, stormy night the moon turned off its lights and went to sleep. Everyone in the Venn house was asleep, except for three friends... James, Jake and Joel. They were clown friends. "Hurry up!" whispered Joel.
They were crawling through the pipes whilst James woke Harry up. "I'm tired, I don't want to have breakfast..." *What! It's twelve-thirty at night. Why is Mum waking me up?* "What was that? Dad this isn't funny."
"Hehe!"
"Ooooo!" said James. James was very good at impressions.
"Argh! Mum?" shouted Harry.
Harry's mum and dad were clowns!

Harry Venn (10)
North Newton Community Primary School, North Newton

THE GHOST

I was sleeping but when I woke up I heard something that was very loud and scary. It sounded like Lego breaking so I took a peek as I thought it was a ghost. I thought, *I have to get to the light switch.* I lifted my duvet off of me and I crept to my wardrobe. I heard rustling and a cute whimpering sound and I gently pushed open the door. To my surprise, there was my dog, Clover, who is adorable, just chewing my Lego!

Hamish Hendry (9)
Millfield Preparatory School, Glastonbury

DEATH UPON DEATH

Death lives, breathes, takes and kills. Innocent souls loom and idle in his void, moaning and groaning, staring at their past, wondering what the future is like. Death never dies, it stays alive, we all go to his void and feel the pain he creates and musters, he strikes in the night and pulls the life out of us and drags us to death. If you defeat Death, you have glory, faith and dreams as high as a mountain, a drive to push, but Death will catch you eventually.

Victoria Baughan (10)
Millfield Preparatory School, Glastonbury

THE ATTIC

One day, my mum and I were cleaning up the house so Mum said to go clean up the attic. I climbed up the ladder and stood up and in the darkness I thought I saw a shadow. I turned around and saw a doll. The doll was on a rocking horse. It started to move and float towards me. The eyes opened, it was coming at me so quickly I thought it would knock me over! Then, Mum, she saved me because she popped her head up and the doll stopped. "Mum, I found your old doll."

Erin Joy Catt (9)
Millfield Preparatory School, Glastonbury

THE MONSTER UPON MONSTER

Erin is a vampire, Margot is a ghost, Aggie is a witch and I am dressed up as a monster. We are just leaving my warm bedroom going into the dark to trick or treat. Suddenly, we hear footsteps above. There is someone in the attic. The ladder comes crashing down but there is nobody so we climb up. The steps creak and we can see a moonlit attic and a chair rocking. Why? Who? We pray it isn't a ghost but a black cat brushes against my legs and runs into the fog. It is my black cat, Tom.

Francesca Cooper (9)
Millfield Preparatory School, Glastonbury

MY BIKE

The first morning I woke up at the farm I saw a smiling scarecrow in the field.
That night I heard noises outside. I looked out the window but it was dark and foggy. I couldn't see the scarecrow. I went for a walk to see what had made the noise. The scarecrow was now standing near my bike in my front garden wearing a creepy look. I ran to my bedroom and hid under the covers.
When I woke up it was sunny. There was no scarecrow in the garden or in the field and my bike had gone.

Caleb Gifford-Groves (9)
Millfield Preparatory School, Glastonbury

THE MOST TERRIFYING!

Suddenly I find myself in a forbidden forest in the middle of nowhere. The trees are moving, it's pitch-black. The floor is muddy, the sky is plain. Wait, what... I hear something. What, wait. I hear it again, is it a ghost or is it a monster? I don't know, this is terrifying! I have to face my fears so I look around. A shadow moves beneath the trees, a shadow of some sort of weird shape. The shape of a creature of some sort. Then, when I look again, it spots me... "Vampire!"

Cecily Lewis (9)
Millfield Preparatory School, Glastonbury

THE NIGHT OF THE GHOST

On Halloween, I went trick or treating. When I got to the top of the hill I saw a big, big, scary house. I took a big deep breath and walked up to the front door. I rang the doorbell and the door opened slowly and squeakily. I walked in, the floorboards creaked. I was horrified to see a baby ghost in the corner, it was moaning. The ghost floated and said, "Follow me," in a whispering voice. It took me to a table laden with all the sweets I could think of. It said, "Take anything you want."

Brianna Davies (9)
Millfield Preparatory School, Glastonbury

THE CREEPY HOUSE

Bob was going trick or treating. He went to a house. When he rang the doorbell the door magically opened so he stepped inside. The door shut with a bang! Bob was afraid of the house because the floor was slipping and some of the planks were missing. From the misty darkness, a creepy monster emerged with a gulping eye. Bob started to run, he kept on running until he lost the monster. Then he found an exit but the monster amazingly found him. He got caught, then woke up. It was all just a dream. "Phew!"

Leon Hutchcroft (9)
Millfield Preparatory School, Glastonbury

THE VAMPIRE TERROR

Once there was a vampire who loved scaring people that came in his haunted house. The vampire usually popped his head off and put it right in their faces.

One time a bunch of tourists came in to check if it was scary enough to make people run for their stupid lives. The vampire knew he had scared them so much, so he shut the door but the people didn't know that, so he got a little scared. The vampire came out and popped his head off and the people who were judging ran away and screamed for their lives.

Aman Tinubu (9)
Millfield Preparatory School, Glastonbury

THE STARTLING NIGHT

It was gloomy but moonlit when I went for a stroll. This night was so sinisterly quiet my whole body shook. As I shuffled forward a scuffle stopped me in my tracks. I spun around and then gasped with relief for it was just a squirrel scurrying by. I ran on quickening my pace, but when I suddenly saw a looming figure in the dark I screamed with fright. It had grotesque long horns. I shone my torch and a bemused deer galloped away. Then heading back home I saw it... not a deer but a monster! "Uh-oh!"

Tiffany Harbridge (9)
Millfield Preparatory School, Glastonbury

WHO'S THERE?

"Lily, can you go up to the attic to get Dad's old clown toy?" shouted Mum.

"Okay, Mum."

Lily went up to the attic. When she got up to the attic Lily's dad walked by the attic and he shut the attic steps but Lily did not see him shut the attic. Once Lily had found the clown toy she went back to the attic steps, but they weren't there anymore. Lily dropped the clown toy but when she went back to pick it up it was gone... Lily heard voices. In the end, it was just her mum.

Aggie Eve Stamper (9)
Millfield Preparatory School, Glastonbury

NEVER AGAIN!

Jeff went down into the dark, damp cellar. Bob shut the door and it automatically locked. He felt scared, cold and thirsty. He reached out to get a beer. Something touched him. He jumped back in fear. The thing that touched him said, "I'm coming to get you!"
He fainted as he was frightened. Then he felt a slimy, cold thing on his face and something scratched his head. He then heard heavy breathing like a train. He got up, it was only Bob, his dog. Never again would he go into the cellar to get a beer!

Archie Monk (9)
Millfield Preparatory School, Glastonbury

FAMILY SCARES

Once there was a girl called Lily, who went upstairs to find something about her family history. Whilst rummaging she found a big dusty book called 'My Family'. Whilst flicking through the pages she looked at the pictures very closely and all of the names. She was getting too scared now so she ran down to her mum and dad who were making tea. She noticed her mum and dad were a witch and a vampire. Lily thought, *this is just like the book I read.* Then Lily was way too scared so she ran and locked herself away.

Adriana Richard (9)
Millfield Preparatory School, Glastonbury

THE UNDERWORLD!

Claudia ran away from a fire. No one knew how it started. She ran so hard that she didn't see the open tomb and fell in! Some spooky figure that had no marks came towards her and said, "Hello Claudia!"
She was so spooked that she let out a scream. Then she realised it was her best friend, Moma! Moma had been missing for twelve years but now this was her chance to come back alive. The spirit sent them both back up to the living world. When they arrived Claudia returned Moma to her parents and she found hers!

Scarlet Oliver (9)
Millfield Preparatory School, Glastonbury

THE GHOUL

A dark and stormy night, the trees were blowing and houses were falling down behind Jake, he was getting chased by a ghoul. It was knocking down everything in its path. Jake was used to getting chased by monsters but not like this. There was blood dripping down its eyes and it was floating like a ghost. He was hiding in his village church but suddenly, Jake heard a noise. He wanted to peek outside but he knew it could lead to very big consequences. He peeked outside anyway, it was a man, but hang on, what happened to him...

Barnaby Fairweather (9)
Millfield Preparatory School, Glastonbury

WHO IS IT?

One stormy night I go to bed. I'm tucked in and my mum turns the lights off and leaves to go downstairs. I hear noises outside my room and I say to myself, "Who is it? It can't be my parents, they are downstairs. Who is it?"
The room is terrifyingly dark and chilling. Then my door opens and I see a figure. "Who is it?" I say nervously. It stands still for a second. Who can it be? It's coming towards me, it's still walking in my direction. I turn on my light. "Hello!" It is my dad.

Seth Collins (9)
Millfield Preparatory School, Glastonbury

THE MONSTER MYSTERY!

I jumped into bed, switched my lamp off. The bed shook violently. I called down to my parents. No answer. I decided to peek under my bed. "Argh!" I saw two bloodshot eyes. Red shaking ones. I jumped out of bed. I heard ferocious growling. What very strange monster would growl like that? A furry hand touched my shoulder gently. Wet sticky slobber dripped onto my back. "Argh!" It was so scary. Wait a moment, that black hairy face... It was my pet dog, Bolt. He had scared me so much. That was so freaky. What a relief!

Isla R Shelver (9)
Millfield Preparatory School, Glastonbury

THE FORBIDDEN FOREST

There was once a boy who dreamed of taking over Chepstow; he longed to rule The Forbidden Forest. He planned to contaminate the people, but he doubted that they would listen to him. So, he tested the gas on his friends, those who listened became contaminated - changed to zombies. These zombies soon began to bite all those who lived in the forest. But, after 24 hours, the gas wore off and the original person returned. However, if the creator gets bitten by a zombie, he will never be cured, but does the creator still lurk in The Forbidden Forest?

Joe Tucker (10)
Millfield Preparatory School, Glastonbury

CHLOE'S SPOOKY ATTIC

One stormy night, a little girl named Chloe was fast asleep in bed when she had a bad dream. There was a witch in her dream and it said, "Chloe, don't come in the attic, it has a secret you don't want to see."
Chloe suddenly woke up. "I just had the weirdest dream," she said to herself. "I'm just going to get a drink." But when Chloe went to get a drink from the kitchen, as she was going down the stairs, she noticed a bright green light, just visible through the attic door, so she followed it...

Lottie Raby-Brown (10)
Millfield Preparatory School, Glastonbury

SPOOKY, SCARY SPIDERS

It was time for bed on a very windy and cold night. Outside the gusty wind made the wheelie bin rattle. Zen became scared and looked outside and said, "What was that noise?" Instead of an answer, he heard more of the scary noise. It came from the ceiling and slowly Zen looked up and saw webs, everywhere on the webs were hairy nightmares with eight legs and there were about a hundred of them. They came on his face. He screamed, "Help!" but he had already woken up.
His mum came and said, "What? Did you have a nightmare?"

Zen Kaart (9)
Millfield Preparatory School, Glastonbury

THE BLOB

There were just bones all over the gloomy, dark stair box through the broken wall. Seth walked down the stairs interested by why the skeletons were in his house. He followed a shiny, glowing blob which was leaving a golden trail on the pitch-black floor. He found at least one hundred glowing blobs. How did they get here? One followed him off the pile, Seth backed away very slowly but the blob kept on following him. The blob disintegrated into the bones of the skeleton. The skeleton started to move towards Seth. The door locked.
Seth woke up screaming.

Jem Hedgcock (9)
Millfield Preparatory School, Glastonbury

THE MISSING DOLL

Taylor tossed his forgotten doll into the smelly garbage bin. What he did not realise was the doll was alive. Taylor wondered what the creaking sound was and why the mysterious shadows fell. It was the missing doll, but why did it look so hideous? It had blood dripping all over, fur protruding from its gory body and looked horrendous. It was coming closer to his bed. It hurled itself onto his bed lacerating his duvet. It wrestled his pillows, scratched his six-pack. There were bloodstains everywhere. Suddenly, his mum walked in and as if by magic it vanished.

Taylor Powell (9)
Millfield Preparatory School, Glastonbury

THE DARK DIMENSION

Hallah the Destroyer is the arch-nemesis of Valhalla the Creator. The only thing that can keep them apart is the haunted ghost. The ghost keeps them apart by keeping them in the Dark Dimension.

One day, something terrible happened. Hallah, using his god-like powers obliterated the barrier to the human world. He landed in the Manson Crater, Iowa, USA and doubled the size of the crater. After he found out it was so boring on Earth, he tried to get back up but he couldn't get to the opening.

After time, he changed to human form and the rift closed.

Osbert William Norby Weston (9)
Millfield Preparatory School, Glastonbury

THE NEW HOUSE

One very dark and spooky night, Alex and his parents arrived at their new home by the farm. They were very tired so they rapidly inflated the mattresses and took their dog for a walk. Suddenly, one of the scarecrows turned its head and gazed at Alex until finally, Alex realised he was being watched. He slowly turned around and saw the scarecrow right behind him. "Argh!" Alex shouted at the top of his voice.

At that moment his parents came bursting into the room asking, "What's the matter?"

Then he realised that it was just a dream.

Alex Major (10)
Millfield Preparatory School, Glastonbury

A SPOOKY SURPRISE

It was a dark and stormy night, the wind was howling. Rafael struggled to open the car door against the force of the wind. When he stepped out into the cold night, he felt panic-stricken. His arms got goosebumps as he crept slowly towards the building. As he progressed he noticed shadows dancing on the pavement, like a giant hand clawing at him. He nervously turned around and was grateful to find that it was a bare tree. He finally reached the building and nervously opened the old oak door. It creaked open and he peered inside... "Surprise! Happy birthday!"

Brychan James (10)
Millfield Preparatory School, Glastonbury

A WALK IN THE FOREST

One day, a ten-year-old girl, Lucy, was walking her puppy, Coco, out in the forest behind her garden. Coco started barking, then started to run. Coco then ran into a bramble bush and started whining. Lucy dropped down and found no brambles at all in Coco's fur. "What's up Coco?" Lucy now saw why Coco was whining. A big, tall figure was leaning over them.
"Hello," said a misty voice.
Lucy then saw what she thought was blood dribbling from their pocket. Lucy slowly looked up and realised that it was her mum who had been picking berries.

Georgiana Harriet Gordon (9)
Millfield Preparatory School, Glastonbury

SURPRISE

A dark, windy night, a girl called Erin was walking alone in the dark. She saw a creepy house and she walked into it, she touched something. She thought, *what is it? It is soft and it has a tail.* She needed the light but she couldn't see anything. She was so scared, so she just walked past. She touched another thing, it was a handle. She opened the door and heard something. She checked under the bed but there was nothing under it.
Bang!
"Argh!" Erin screamed. It was Aggie, Erin's best friend.
"Ha ha, I scared you."

Dora Ji (9)
Millfield Preparatory School, Glastonbury

THE HOUSE WITH THE BIG BLACK DOOR

It was a stormy Halloween afternoon and the weather was wild. Three friends called Sophie, Tiffany and Ffion had dressed up as witches. They were walking around the village knocking on doors for trick or treats. At one house the big black door opened silently, swinging open as they knocked. It was very dark inside and the girls felt frightened. They slowly crept inside the blackness. Suddenly, the door slammed shut behind them and the girls screamed. "Argh!" Sophie quickly switched on the torch, Tiffany grabbed the door handle and opened the door. They ran out into the night.

Sophie Angelosanto (9)
Millfield Preparatory School, Glastonbury

THE CREEPY DOLL

Creak! Jack opens his eyes, he's in the attic and it's still pitch-black. He looks to the side - there's an empty sleeping bag. His friend Andrew is gone. *Creak!* Jack hears it again. A voice says, "Can you play with me?"
"Hello?" he whispers.
Jack feels a chill on his shoulder. Terrified, he gets up and moves forward. Jack opens the door. He sees his sister's doll lying on the floor. Jack's hands shake; his throat is dry. He picks it up and again he hears, "Can you play with me?" as his sister walks out of the bathroom.

Oona Knight (9)
Millfield Preparatory School, Glastonbury

THE NOISE?

My mum went into the attic to put some books away. Then the door slammed shut. She needed help! Suddenly, she heard a voice.
"Ooooh... ooooh."
"Help!" she yelled. "Help! Help! Help!" She saw something moving. "Help! Help!"
Downstairs my dad heard a noise coming from the attic. Mum looked around. There was nothing until she turned around and she saw a doll drop! She screamed! *Bump!* Dad burst through the door! Mum pointed to the doll. Dad laughed as a mouse came out of the doll. As Mum and Dad left the attic the doll's creepy eyes suddenly opened...

Ffion Lockley (9)
Millfield Preparatory School, Glastonbury

THE MIRRORED REFLECTION

Twice upon a time, there was a young girl called Petunia. She had blonde hair and brown eyes.
One day, she went up to her attic. As she was opening a box, she heard a moan from inside another box... "Hello?" she said. It came closer.
"Hi! I'm Julian. I need a friend."
"Okay."
"I need to eat you!"
"Eek!"
Petunia took a sharp turn across the attic. Wait, had this happened before? She ran. She woke up. This was all a dream... or was it an actual dream?
Then, Mother came in. "Petunia, you were sleeping in the daytime..."

Amelia Greatrex (9)
Millfield Preparatory School, Glastonbury

THE SPOOKY SHED

I walked to the shed under the light of a shimmering moon, I went in. *Crunch, crunch, crunch.* The door locked behind me, the light flashed on and off. A scary voice screeched, "Drink me."
I slowly drank the drink and to my surprise, nothing happened. Suddenly, many voices surrounded me.
"Help me."
"Eat me."
"Argh!" I screamed. The light started to shine brightly, I couldn't see, I was blind. Something cold and slimy pushed me into a chair, then tied me down. I couldn't move, I couldn't breathe. I started screaming, "Help me!" How was I going to escape?

Sian Davies (9)
Millfield Preparatory School, Glastonbury

THE MONSTER CAME ALIVE!

In the graveyard a little kid came out dressed like a vampire, then a fish came out and started to dance and it made every kid laugh. It was only a kid dressed as a fish but he only wanted attention because he never got attention. He only ever got his Mum's attention and he hated that. The only thing he liked was the attention but he didn't mean to scare all of the children. He just wanted them to laugh. All of the monsters were just all of the children.

Lilly Moss (7)
Milford Junior School, Yeovil

THE STORY OF THE HAUNTED HOUSE

Once, there was a little girl called Annabelle. She was walking through the woods. She saw a haunted, abandoned house that had a lot of spiderwebs. Annabelle went into the house. She saw lots of things move. The haunted house used to be a museum 100 years ago. All the glass was broken and covered in blood. She was so scared that she ran away to the end of the woods. When she was at the end she looked around and saw her home. She ran and never looked back. That was the last time Annabelle went into the woods.

Lacey Smith (7)
Milford Junior School, Yeovil

THE GHOST IN THE ATTIC

Once upon a time, there were two boys, Charlie and Jack. They lived with their mother, Cally. One day, they were all invited to their auntie's house to have dinner and help sort out their holiday photos. When they arrived Cally and Auntie Ruby sent the boys to the attic while they had coffee and a chat. Charlie and Jack ran up the stairs very excited. They burst through the door and standing in front of them was... a ghost! The boys stood still and the ghost said, "Thank you. You have unlocked the spell." Then he disappeared.

Chloe Hale-Sanders (7)
Milford Junior School, Yeovil

THE SCARY MANSION

There was a house and a boy called Josh. He had a mum but she went to work so Josh went trick or treating with his friends and he saw a big mansion. He was all alone because his friends went home so he went in the mansion and it was dark. He saw a candle and lit it up and went upstairs. He saw a big room with cobwebs and there was dust everywhere. One second later, this man popped out and said, "Roar!" The little boy screamed forever.

Casie-Jade Chubb (9)
Charlton Mackrell CE Primary School, Charlton Mackrell

ZOMBIE TEACHERS

Tom, a 12-year-old kid hated school, he thought his teachers acted strangely. Once when he went to school something terrible happened. A new kid came to school, he was so smart that at break time he was given special treatment. Tom was curious so he followed them. They took him to the office. Tom looked in, he saw the teachers turn into zombies and eat the child, but then they saw Tom. They chased him, he slipped on a bin lid and they ate him. *Munch, munch.*

George Chevis (9)
Charlton Mackrell CE Primary School, Charlton Mackrell

BIG SHADOW

The door slammed behind me! I could hear rustling under the fire. As the shadow on the wall was getting bigger and bigger I felt like I was going to be sick and I scrambled under the table covered in goosebumps. I tried to call my parents but there was no signal due to the thunderstorm outside. I heard police sirens and made a quick dash out of the door. I sprinted to the police as fast as I could. The police went into the room and found nothing but as they left a little mouse ran straight past them!

Sam Butler (9)
Charlton Mackrell CE Primary School, Charlton Mackrell

THE WEIRD AND SCARY CORRIDOR

As I walked down the dark and creepy corridor I suddenly heard a noise behind me. I turned around to see a figure standing there. It must have been about ten foot high. I was frozen in fear as doors slammed around me and windows swung open. The thing started to walk towards me, its boots clumping along the corridor. I tried to run but something was holding me back. As the figure reached me I tried to scream but nothing came out, only a little whisper. When the thing reached me it said to me, "You will die!"

Peter Robinson O'Boyle (10)
Charlton Mackrell CE Primary School, Charlton Mackrell

ABANDONED PRISON

Bob and the cameraman entered the abandoned prison filming their latest video. They thought they were ready for anything but the deathly silence put them on edge. Suddenly, they heard a toilet flush from inside a cell. They realised they were not alone. What were they to do? There was no way out without passing the cell. As they crept past they heard a spooky laugh. They were really scared now. Bob decided to enter the cell! In the corner of the cell Bob saw a skeleton. With a loud scream, they turned and ran for their lives.

Scarlet Adams (8)
Charlton Mackrell CE Primary School, Charlton Mackrell

SHIVER

It was 1902 and there was a little girl called Victoria. She walked past a house she'd never seen before so she went in and realised the wallpaper was still hanging onto the wall. She looked around to see if anyone was there. She thought no one was there but there was. She went upstairs after seeing the kitchen. It had rats. "Yuck!" she said. She went upstairs only to realise there was someone there. She saw a long figure peering over her. "Argh! Help me." Victoria was scared. "Help me!" Victoria was dead.

Isobel Carrick (8)
Charlton Mackrell CE Primary School, Charlton Mackrell

MONSTERS IN THE CUPBOARD

Once upon a time, in Monster City, a scary monster appeared in the brown cupboard of an attic in a creepy, abandoned house which was haunted. He opened the old squeaky door, to his left there was a bucket of blood and monsters' eyeballs and worms mushed up. There was a bed randomly.
He looked under the bed. He was so scared. All he could see was loads of earwigs and woodlouse. "Oh wait, is that a monster?" He screamed so loud a window broke. It was a monster... a monster with green fangs, one arm and razor-sharp teeth...

Jude Ray Elston (9)
Charlton Mackrell CE Primary School, Charlton Mackrell

KETCHUP CATASTROPHE

One day, a boy called Bob and his cat named Twiglet went on an adventure to an eerie, creepy, abandoned house which was haunted. They opened the creaky door which led to a dark and cold hallway. The door slammed behind them. They heard a weird howling from upstairs. They went up the creaky and smelly stairs. They thought the smell was blood but the blood smell was actually tomato ketchup. What they thought was the ghost was actually the wind that was blowing the curtains around which knocked over the tomato ketchup. Bob and Twiglet went home for Ted.

David Fraser (9)
Charlton Mackrell CE Primary School, Charlton Mackrell

MR WOLFIE AND THE MANIC ATTACK

It started on a movie set but then it spread. Filming had started. The cast and crew of Mr Wolfie were just packing up when they heard a piercing howl. An ominous shadow appeared behind them. Mr Wolfie had come to life. Panic spread across the set as he crept closer. Suddenly, the deafening roar of a chainsaw ripped through the air. The maniac chainsaw clown had chopped off Mr Wolfie's head. There was a river of blood across the floor and the maniac chainsaw clown emerged from behind the trailer, it was grinning at everyone as it started giggling.

Evie Burrell (11)
Charlton Mackrell CE Primary School, Charlton Mackrell

THE HAUNTED HOUSE

One day, a girl called Sophie was moving into a new house. She kept on hearing strange and eerie noises that made her suspicious. Sophie told her mum about the eerie noises. She said they would go and investigate.
After many days of investigating they kept finding footprints going into the cellar...
The next day, Sophie and her mum crept into the cellar. The footprints became more clear. They wondered what or who it could be. They got more nervous as they went further into the cellar and then heard a big bang but no one knew who it was.

Imogen Grace Baker (10)
Charlton Mackrell CE Primary School, Charlton Mackrell

MYSTERY IN THE CUPBOARD

I'm in my room trying to get my clothes for school. Suddenly, I'm pulled into the cupboard, the door closes. I attempt to open it but it's locked! I try to open it again but it's jammed shut! Behind me, an object moves, crawling across the floor. "Is it me or is my shirt alive?" A white shadow lurks behind the shirt. "It's a ghost!" The ghost charges at me but instead of hurting me he gives me a big hug. Then I realise it's my white, wonderful pet cat named Snowflake and it's not a nasty ghost. "Phew!"

Jimi Barclay (9)
Charlton Mackrell CE Primary School, Charlton Mackrell

THE ABANDONED HUT

This ordinary day was about to be twisted. Amy and her BFF, Jessica, were strolling along when they saw a narrow path leading to an old hut. After they had a look around they started to head for the door, then it flung itself shut. The lights started to flicker. A breeze brushed past them. All of a sudden, a tall figure appeared. Jessica and Amy screamed, "Argh!" Jessica then stopped screaming. She had disappeared. Amy ran for the door but it wouldn't open. "Would you like to play with me?" came a small voice that sounded too familiar.

Jemima Carrick (11)
Charlton Mackrell CE Primary School, Charlton Mackrell

THE RETURN OF THE SPIRITS!

One sunny day, there lived a girl called Juliet who had a best friend called Chelsea.
On Friday night, Chelsea and Juliet were having a sleepover, but it wasn't an ordinary Friday because it was Friday the thirteenth. That night Juliet and Chelsea were eating pizza when they saw a Coke bottle move on its own, then behind they saw a creepy vampire and he weirdly said, "I am Harvey the spirit wizard and I am going to..." Then he suddenly shouted, "Eat all your cheese pizza!"
They both rolled their eyes and said, "I was enjoying that!"

Chelsea David (11)
Charlton Mackrell CE Primary School, Charlton Mackrell

THE WHISPER IS COMING!

In a land where monsters, ghosts and vampires existed, there was a girl called Sam, she was trick or treating by herself. She came across a gloomy-looking church which was glowing. She looked in and called, "Hello?" No answer. She went in leaving her sweets by the gate.
Sam walked down the path getting closer to the church when suddenly she heard a whisper, "Come to me."
Sam got scared and started running towards the gate.
"It's locked!"
Sam yelled. "Help!"
The whisper said, "There's nowhere to run."
"Help!"
Silence. To this day it still remains a mystery.

Matilda Stothard (9)
Charlton Mackrell CE Primary School, Charlton Mackrell

THE NURSE

One day, a boy went to hospital. He walked in and found the lights were off. He still looked for an ice pack. He went into the nursery room and found the light on. He went into one of the refrigerators and found an ice pack and headed out but the door was locked.

He woke on a bed finding a nurse walking out; he followed her into a room of bodies and saw one key in a mouth. He grabbed the key and went to the front door and unlocked it but the nurse came and killed him.

Harvey Leonard Jenkins (11)
Catcott Primary School, Catcott

BOB IN THE WOODS

Bob was in the woods trying to find a home and an old man who lived in there. Bob found this caravan and he found it rather comfortable. He fell asleep. Then an alien tapped him on the shoulder and Bob woke up. There was nothing there. He went outside and looked around and an alien tapped him on the shoulder. Then the alien gave him a picture of the caravan in flames. He looked at the caravan on fire and the alien disappeared. Bob then found his way home and told his mum but she'd seen it all!

Liam King (11)
Catcott Primary School, Catcott

THE LANDLORD

Sam, lost in the woods, found a landlord who bought a farm ruin and said that he could stay. He walked up the driveway and saw the farmhouse undamaged. He opened the door and saw a woman and a dog. "I have room for you and some roast," said the woman.
When he'd finished the roast she gave him a cake. He was full so he put it in his bag and went to bed.
At dawn, he went to thank the landlord for sending her. The landlord told Sam that he didn't send anyone. Did Sam find a ghoul?

Keira Hadfield (10)
Catcott Primary School, Catcott

THE HAUNTED HOSPITAL!

A boy was trekking in Taunton; he fell outside an eerie derelict house… He yelped, "Help!" A weird man picked him up and brought him in, he was freaked out. *Is it a hospital?* he thought. He got into bed, he fell asleep, woke up and wanted a drink but he could not pick his cup up. He needed the toilet but saw flying people, his leg felt better so he went outside as he felt healthier. Could they see him or not? Could they hear him or not? He was worried. What do you think happened next?

Barnaby Cosser (10)
Catcott Primary School, Catcott

MURDEROUS SKIING

One night, Alex was skiing down the Himalayas when a snowstorm began. Alex had to find shelter. He discovered a cave which strangely had a torch lit inside. He walked further into the cave and saw a white glow. Alex walked around the corner and caught sight of Hitler and 18 of his soldiers all with muskets and blades. Alex started running but tripped on a rock, all 19 ghosts started chasing after him. He was hit by one of the pellets and he lay on the floor wounded. The ghosts stabbed him till he was definitely dead.

Robbie Armstrong (10)
Catcott Primary School, Catcott

THE HAUNTED DOLL

George went down his childhood lane, he saw a man standing by a sign waiting for someone to rent his house. George asked the man if he could and the man said yes.
The next night, he was handed the key and made his way down the path towards the house. He went to the door, walked in and went upstairs to unpack. He walked downstairs and found a doll sitting with a knife. George ran to the man. "George, you need to burn it otherwise bad things will happen."
It was too late, he didn't get there in time.

Jemima Lush (11)
Catcott Primary School, Catcott

THE GHOST OF MR CLENCH

In 1942, a British soldier was wounded in the leg and called for help. His best friend, Tom Clench, saw him and carried him behind the lines to an old trench. They slid into the squelchy mud but Tom spotted a mountain of old German corpses. He put his friend down to investigate. Then they spotted a German soldier, Tom was about to shoot when the man fell dead, but then poor Tom was scratched down the back and died. What was it? Tom was never seen again, though his surviving comrades say that he still haunts that trench now.

Caleb Masters (11)
Catcott Primary School, Catcott

THE HAUNTED BOOKS!

Twice upon a time, a 16-year-old boy, Zack, who searched for a place to stay, eventually found a place. As he went to turn the iron key, the dim moonlight shone and lit up the old, dull, grey house. As he settled in he lent on a brick that revealed... a hidden bookshelf with tons of books: 'How to Kill a Monster', 'Night of the Living Dummy', all from the Goosebumps' series. Next to them was a key. The third book became unlocked and the innocent words leapt off the page into something far more sinister.

Ewan Robinson (10)
Catcott Primary School, Catcott

BRUISES

Every night I wake up covered in bruises. I've told Mum, she says it's sleepwalking. It's concerning I always wake up in the same place. One night, at midnight, I wake up to see two ghostly hands dangling from the ceiling. I start to panic while I am being grabbed and bruised. I scream for Mum and she bursts into my room. She tells me to stay still and stay on the bed. Finally, she tells me what is happening. There used to be a child that fell out his window and died. They buried the baby under the floorboards!

Lola Smith (10)
Catcott Primary School, Catcott

THE GRAVEYARD AND THE SPIRITS

Mr Lock always looked out his windows to check on the graveyard and to check that nothing was stolen.
One night, he spied a broken grave. No human could have broken it, it was made of stone. It wasn't a natural crack. Then he made some cocoa and went to bed. He had forgotten everything by the morning, then throughout the day, Mr Lock started to put up the Halloween decorations for Wednesday.
When he went to bed all the dead spirits rose. They formed a ghoulish shadow. It managed to get inside. What did it do to Mr Lock?

Seren Richards (10)
Catcott Primary School, Catcott

WHERE AM I?

John woke, confused he sat up, his face drained, colourless. He looked around. He attempted the front door, of course, locked. He tried the window when a slow creak interrupted him. Was someone following him? He hurriedly checked all drawers, no key. He realised he hadn't eaten in days. He started looking for food. John noticed a pie. As he gobbled up the pie a key fell from the crust, he had found the key. He ran outside but fell unconscious for an hour. He woke and realised that there was no house yet. He still had the golden key.

Aerron Karma (10)
Catcott Primary School, Catcott

THE VICTORIAN DOLL

Millie bought a holiday home. It was a Victorian house. She saw her house but thought it was slightly unusual. The windows glowed with light. Millie navigated her way through the dark hallways, to find the kitchen. She heard laughter and haunting screams but tried to comfort herself. Millie froze in the doorway and saw a ghostly figure gliding through the kitchen. She ushered Millie in. Seven girls skipped into the kitchen playing. She quickly returned the key and explained the ghosts. Millie took a pale doll and an ear-piercing scream echoed through the house...

Thalia MacLeay (11)
Catcott Primary School, Catcott

ASWANG!

A Hooke soldier patrols a creepy town made of wooden huts. It's ghostly, dingy and eerie. He begins to settle when he finds natives. Are they dead or alive? The question fills up his mind. Suddenly, he feels a rush of cold air. He isn't alone. What's with him then? He suddenly spots a black silhouette, it has eyes as red as a demon's, its back is bent low, its fangs are dripping with drool. "Aswang!" the Hooke screeches.
Suddenly, there is a rupturing sound.
The next day, a Hooke patrol finds gashes and finds a body drained of blood.

Jim Young (10)
Catcott Primary School, Catcott

THE WAILING ZOMBIE

Sophie stood waiting outside her house in the cold darkness, her bag hung heavily on her, she had brought way too much to her sleepover! Sophie could hear a zombie wailing in the distance. She ran as fast as a cheetah but then tripped and crashed to the ground. Sophie screamed. Had the zombie got her? She stood up straight and still, feeling her painful knee. She felt warm blood dripping. In the distance a small light shone, it came closer and closer... Sophie was scared. She stood motionless. The light shone on Sophie's face. "Hi Sophie," said her friend.

Rosie Ramsay (9)
Catcott Primary School, Catcott

NUMBER NINE NORTHBROOK DRIVE

Ella's wandering around the countryside. She seeks refuge in an old house. It looks derelict but she knocks on the door. A soft voice says, "Come in!"
She enters, walks into the front room and relaxes on the sofa. Three-year-old twins toddle into the room followed by a young man and woman carrying a tray of food. Ella doesn't think how they know she's hungry. She stays one night and takes selfies before saying farewell. She bumps into the mayor and congratulates her on friendly families like number nine. She says the family died; Ella shows selfies...

Alice King (10)
Catcott Primary School, Catcott

THE DEVIL'S HOUR

He knocked on my door again. Tears streamed down my face. "Go away!" I shouted, curling into the blanket. He knocked louder. It was 3am. He always came at this hour on the dot, I thought it was my brother knocking to prank me until my parents said he went missing earlier this morning.
"Open the door, Kate!"
"Callum, is it really you?" I shouted, throwing the covers off me and pressing my ear to the door.
"Yes!"
I opened the door, the lights flickered, blood was splattered across the walls spelling the word 'run'. Was this the end?

Jasmine Rose Lawrence (9)
Catcott Primary School, Catcott

THE KILLER CARAVAN

One weekend in mid-October, Molly and Mason were bored so they asked their parents if they could meet up at their local woods. After walking for ages, they stumbled across Mason's gran's exhausted caravan which his Grandad died in. Because they'd been wanting to camp out for ages, they decided to find Mason's gran's keys but soon after they returned to smashed windows. On the sofa, there she was, a doll, staring up at them with her beady eyes. After sleeping on their nightmare, Mason's gran arrived to take a look. She turned pale. "That, that's, that's her."

Izzy Campion (10)
Catcott Primary School, Catcott

THE ROOM!

Once upon a time, there was a little girl who lived with her dad. Sadly her mum had died. They lived in a haunted house. Her dad said, "Do not go in that room."
One night, she went in the room... She was grabbed. She tried to scream but the monster was too strong. Finally, she screamed and her dad came in the room and she was saved. Afterwards, they moved out!

Brayden Carl John Fitzgerald (8)
Bishop Henderson CE Primary School, Taunton

THE GHOST THAT CHANGED SAHRA'S LIFE

There was a girl called Sahra who moved to a different town with her dad. She played tricks on people and they did not like it so people stopped believing her.
One day a house was making sounds so Sahra checked it out. *Bang!* There was a noise upstairs so she went up and, "Boo!" There was a ghost. She screamed but nobody listened because she always played tricks on people. She ran outside, left the town and never played tricks on people ever again!

Kacey May Fitzgerald (10)
Bishop Henderson CE Primary School, Taunton

NEVER TRICK OR TREAT ON A FULL MOON

It was the night of a full moon. My cousin and I were trick or treating. We had been to 50 houses when we came across a forbidden field with a house in the middle. We knocked on the door and guy shouted, "Go away," but we knocked again. The guy came to the door with a girl. The guy was holding a knife around the girl's neck. He said, "If you don't go away in five seconds I'll kill her."
We didn't move and he slashed her neck and her head was rolling on the floor.

Desiree De Loureiro (10)
Bishop Henderson CE Primary School, Taunton

THE STORY OF CAMP DEATH

Once one Halloween there was a boy called Tim. Tim went trick or treating by himself and got lost in the forest on the way to meet his friends. He realised he was lost and started running. He heard voices screaming and shouting people. Then he saw a camp called 'Camp Death'. Tim didn't read the sign. He stepped right in. He felt hands crawling up his legs. He got dragged under. He screamed and screamed and tried to get back up. The one thing Tim didn't know was he was being dragged to his death!

Annabel Slade (9)
Bishop Henderson CE Primary School, Taunton

THE MUMMY SAGA

Once upon a time, there lived a little mummy called Bob, he was nine years old and had a mum called Ceria. They lived under a bed and they came out at night-time to hunt their prey. A few moments later, when they came back his mum hid from him. He looked left, right, up and down, but he could not see her. She made spooky sounds to scare him away from the box.
Minutes later, she screamed and looked down. Bob then looked in the box and saw his mum.
"Boo!" he shouted.
"Argh!" she screamed.

George Wilson (9)
Bishop Henderson CE Primary School, Taunton

THE SCARY FARM

The moon shone in the night sky. I was out walking to meet my friends at a farm but I went to the wrong location. I felt like the farm was haunted. I heard spooky noises coming from all around the farm. I was so scared I ran around shouting, "Help, help, is anyone there?" but nobody replied. *What am I going to do?* I thought to myself. "Help, help!" I called again. I was so scared I tried to call my friends but nobody answered. Then I saw a black shadow. "Argh!" I screamed but it was just Mum.

Madison Burton (10)
Bishop Henderson CE Primary School, Taunton

THE NOISE AND THE SCREAM

I wake up and then I say to myself, "Where am I?" I look around and I see peeling wallpaper and broken floorboards, not to mention tons of dust.
Suddenly, I hear a piercing scream, I back into a corner scared for my life. Out of nowhere, I hear a deep voice, "Look behind you!"
I swiftly turn my neck. "W-w-what do you want from me?" I say.
"I want your soul and your fear!"
"Not without a fight you won't."
In a flash, I see a swipe across my face then all I see is darkness.

Liam Shorney (10)
Bishop Henderson CE Primary School, Taunton

FLUMPY BLUMP AND THE TERRIFYING MANSION!

Princess Flumpy had moved to a beautiful mansion. When she arrived something weird happened. She took her things upstairs which felt cold. She turned to see a lamp flying across the bedroom. The princess screamed in fright and leapt down the stairs to find the front door wide open. Suddenly, a ghostly figure loomed in front of her and said, "Hello my dear, has something frightened you?"
"Who are you?" she trembled. Turning round she noticed a portrait of Captain Blump on the wall. Realising she was living in a haunted mansion she lived very spookily with her 'visitor'.

Jessica Newbrook (9)
Bishop Henderson CE Primary School, Taunton

THE SPOOKY SAGAS

Saphie-Mae Johnstone (10)   131
Spencer Craig (9)   132
Joshua Kirby (9)   133
Oliver Lock (9)   134
Oscar Povey (10)   135
Jack Knight (10)   136
Will Murphy (9)   137

VLC Primary School, Milton

Rhys Jefferies (10)   138
Kyros Alabaf (9)   139
James Pearce (10)   140
Rhys Murphy (11)   141

Westfield Primary School, Radstock

John Saunders (10)   142
Mya-May Waldron (10)   143
Leilah Jones (10)   144
Lataya Forde (10)   145
Summer Grimes (10)   146
Louis Pride (10)   147
Chloe Cooper (10)   148
Olivia Swift (11)   149
Sennen Jeffery-Bradley (10)   150
Taylor James Willis (11)   151
Caydence Ayling (11)   152
Mason Faraday (10)   153
Connie Raikes (11)   154
Alfie Besser (11)   155
Adele Lansdown (11)   156
Oliver Filer (10)   157
Jamie Cook (10)   158
Chloe Porter (10)   159
Ella May (10)   160
Thomas Andrews (11)   161
Kelsey Hiscocks (10)   162
Harvey Bancroft (11)   163
Eddie Bushnell (10)   164

Osbert William Norby Weston (9)	52
Taylor Powell (9)	53
Jem Hedgcock (9)	54
Zen Kaart (9)	55
Lottie Raby-Brown (10)	56
Joe Tucker (10)	57
Isla R Shelver (9)	58
Seth Collins (9)	59
Barnaby Fairweather (9)	60
Scarlet Oliver (9)	61
Adriana Richard (9)	62
Archie Monk (9)	63
Aggie Eve Stamper (9)	64
Tiffany Harbridge (9)	65
Aman Tinubu (9)	66
Leon Hutchcroft (9)	67
Brianna Davies (9)	68
Cecily Lewis (9)	69
Caleb Gifford-Groves (9)	70
Francesca Cooper (9)	71
Erin Joy Catt (9)	72
Victoria Baughan (10)	73
Hamish Hendry (9)	74

North Newton Community Primary School, North Newton

Harry Venn (10)	75
Jamie Gauld (10)	76
Olivia Contreras (9)	77
Benjamin Murray (10)	78
Richard Robertson (11)	79
Sophie Bult (10)	80
Faye Little (11)	81
Lola Whatley (10)	82
Grace Palmer (11)	83
James Griffiths (11)	84
Libby Quinn (10)	85
Callum Little (10)	86
Jakob Jones (10)	87
Sonny Morris (11)	88
Freya Bult (9)	89
Raiin Walker (11)	90

Brandon Burton (10)	91
Jayjay Hancock (9)	92
Lily Grindrod (9)	93
Laura Shaw (9)	94

St Georges Church School, St Georges

Carys Welch (9)	95
Matthew Ncube (10)	96
Dylan Welch (10)	97
Harry Watts (11)	98
Amie March (10)	99
Jack Edward Weetch (10)	100
Riley Winfield (10)	101
Nicola Walczak (11)	102
Ashton Gilmore (11)	103
Ellie Hawley (11)	104
Bradley Alexander Reynolds (10)	105
Keira Lovell (10)	106
Poppy Siviter (11)	107
Maddison Mansfield (9)	108
Charlie Baxter-James (9)	109
Roxsi Wakzak (9)	110
Gethin Williams (10)	111
Gabi Niec (9)	112
Paige Richardson (10)	113
Max Cooper (10)	114
Maddison Hughes (9)	115
Tamsen Markham (10)	116
Julia Stankiewicz (9)	117
Faith Murray (9)	118
Ariana Hamlin (9)	119
Katie Pinner (9)	120
Isla Connolly (11)	121
Issy Josie Lanning (10)	122
Izabella Hoskin-Love (9)	123
Jorja Wickens (10)	124
Skarlett Wickens (10)	125
Imogen Harris (10)	126
Emma Louise Payne (10)	127
Oliver Beer (11)	128
Henry Zajac (9)	129
Izzy Hawley (9)	130

CONTENTS

Bishop Henderson CE Primary School, Taunton

Jessica Newbrook (9)	1
Liam Shorney (10)	2
Madison Burton (10)	3
George Wilson (9)	4
Annabel Slade (9)	5
Desiree De Loureiro (10)	6
Kacey May Fitzgerald (10)	7
Brayden Carl John Fitzgerald (8)	8

Catcott Primary School, Catcott

Izzy Campion (10)	9
Jasmine Rose Lawrence (9)	10
Alice King (10)	11
Rosie Ramsay (9)	12
Jim Young (10)	13
Thalia MacLeay (11)	14
Aerron Karma (10)	15
Seren Richards (10)	16
Lola Smith (10)	17
Ewan Robinson (10)	18
Caleb Masters (11)	19
Jemima Lush (11)	20
Robbie Armstrong (10)	21
Barnaby Cosser (10)	22
Keira Hadfield (10)	23
Liam King (11)	24
Harvey Leonard Jenkins (11)	25

Charlton Mackrell CE Primary School, Charlton Mackrell

Matilda Stothard (9)	26
Chelsea David (11)	27
Jemima Carrick (11)	28
Jimi Barclay (9)	29
Imogen Grace Baker (10)	30
Evie Burrell (11)	31
David Fraser (9)	32
Jude Ray Elston (9)	33
Isobel Carrick (8)	34
Scarlet Adams (8)	35
Peter Robinson O'Boyle (10)	36
Sam Butler (9)	37
George Chevis (9)	38
Casie-Jade Chubb (9)	39

Milford Junior School, Yeovil

Chloe Hale-Sanders (7)	40
Lacey Smith (7)	41
Lilly Moss (7)	42

Millfield Preparatory School, Glastonbury

Sian Davies (9)	43
Amelia Greatrex (9)	44
Ffion Lockley (9)	45
Oona Knight (9)	46
Sophie Angelosanto (9)	47
Dora Ji (9)	48
Georgiana Harriet Gordon (9)	49
Brychan James (10)	50
Alex Major (10)	51

FOREWORD

Welcome, Reader!

Here at Young Writers our aim is to encourage creativity in children and to inspire a love of the written word. Each competition we create is tailored to the relevant age group, hopefully giving each child the inspiration and incentive to create their own piece of work, whether it's a poem or a short story. We truly believe that seeing their work in print gives pupils a sense of achievement and pride.

For Young Writers' latest nationwide competition, Spooky Sagas, we gave primary school pupils the task of tackling one of the oldest story-telling traditions: the ghost story. However, we added a twist – they had to write it as a mini saga, a story in just 100 words!

These pupils rose to the challenge magnificently and this resulting collection of spooky sagas will certainly give you the creeps! You may meet friendly ghosts or creepy clowns, or be taken on Halloween adventures to haunted mansions and ghostly graveyards!

So if you think you're ready... read on.